Dear

MW00366613

THE
RIGHTEOUS
ROLE OF A
FATHER

DAVID J. RIDGES

Love
Mom

CFI
An Imprint of Cedar Fort, Inc.
Springville, Utah

The cover art of this book was created by Annie Henrie and is entitled "Love's Pure Light."

This is not an official publication of The Church of Jesus Christ of Latter-day Saints. The opinions and views expressed herein belong solely to the author and do not necessarily represent the opinions or views of Cedar Fort, Inc. Permission for the use of sources, graphics, and photos is also solely the responsibility of the author.

ISBN 13: 978-1-4621-1824-3

Published by CFI, an imprint of Cedar Fort, Inc.
2373 W. 700 S., Springville, UT 84663
Distributed by Cedar Fort, Inc., www.cedarfort.com

LIBRARY OF CONGRESS CATALOGING-IN-PUBLICATION DATA

Names: Ridges, David J., author.
Title: The righteous role of a father / David J. Ridges.
Description: Springville, Utah : CFI, an imprint of Cedar Fort, Inc., [2016]
| "2016 | Includes bibliographical references and index. | Description
based on print version record and CIP data provided by publisher; resource
not viewed.
Identifiers: LCCN 2016001883 (print) | LCCN 2015050997 (ebook) | ISBN
9781462126279 (epub, pdf, mobi) | ISBN 9781462118243 (saddlestitch : alk.
paper)
Subjects: LCSH: Fatherhood--Religious aspects--Church of Jesus Christ of
Latter-day Saints. | Church of Jesus Christ of Latter-day
Saints--Doctrines. | Mormon Church--Doctrines.
Classification: LCC BX8643.F3 (print) | LCC BX8643.F3 R54 2016 (ebook) | DDC
248.8/421--dc23
LC record available at http://lccn.loc.gov/2016001883

Cover design by Shawnda T. Craig
Cover design © 2016 Cedar Fort, Inc.
Edited and typeset by Jessica B. Ellingson

Printed in the United States of America

10 9 8 7 6 5 4 3 2 1

Printed on acid-free paper

A PERSONAL NOTE

Many years ago, the wonder and magnificence of being a father settled strongly into my soul in the delivery room as the nurse gently placed our firstborn child into my awaiting arms. A broad smile spread across my face. "I am a father!" I shouted silently to myself. The words thrilled my heart and warmed my whole soul as I proudly carried our new son to the nursery to be weighed and checked over. That joy and satisfaction of fatherhood has continued to multiply and define me in my own mind over the years.

RIGHTEOUS FATHERHOOD

The Lord's plan for righteous fatherhood brings with it supreme joy and deep satisfaction. Of course, there are also attendant worries and anxieties, but perhaps you've noticed that the highest joys in life often come after tasting of trials and concerns. Men who sincerely strive to carry out their God-given role in the family will reap the highest rewards.

The purpose of this booklet is to explore ways to follow the Lord's plan for responsible fatherhood by highlighting and supporting the righteous role of fathers. It is likewise to remind them that men have a God-given instinct or intuition to love, serve, and protect their family members with strength and inspired tenderness. Another important goal of this booklet is to warn and alert men to be vigilant against getting caught up in the pervasive and invasive wiles of the adversary, who is indeed "the father of all lies" (2 Nephi 2:18), as he strives with every means available to him to culturally and environmentally saturate men with defining input that is opposite to the high role, privilege, responsibility, and opportunity of being good fathers.

FATHER'S INTUITION

We speak often of mother's intuition and of maternal instinct, which are part of the divine nature provided to women by God. It seems, though, that we don't hear as much about "paternal instinct," the natural instinct given to men by God to love, provide for, and protect their families. It can well be referred to as "father's intuition." Obviously, there is considerable overlap between mother's intuition and father's intuition, and thus the roles of fathers and mothers vary considerably within each family. In Heavenly Father's plan of happiness for us, these roles work powerfully together to provide a safe and nurturing environment in which children, as well as parents, can grow and progress toward their full divine potential. In "The Family: A Proclamation to the World," given September 23, 1995, by the First Presidency and Quorum of the Twelve, the Lord makes it clear that both fathers and mothers have a divinely appointed role.

> By divine design, fathers are to preside over their families in love and righteousness and are responsible to provide the necessities of life and protection for their families. Mothers are primarily responsible for the nurture of their children. In these sacred responsibilities, fathers and mothers are obligated to help one another as equal partners.

Here we see that the Father gave each of His spirit daughters and each of His spirit sons complementary roles and feelings designed to strengthen each other and their earthly family units. This can ultimately lead, through worthiness, to eternal family units in which the highest happiness and satisfaction will reside forever.

When fathers realize and deeply feel their privilege as partners with God and their wives in providing Christ-centered homes for their children, a pleasant sense of opportunity and responsibility takes root deep within their souls and continues growing. Their role as a father consistently defines them. It is always there in the background of their minds. It provides perspective and extra incentive to maintain self-control and provide a righteous example. It brings motivation to keep wife and children as top priorities in their daily living. They go out of their way to do so. As providers, nurturers, and protectors, the warmth and light of responsible fatherhood glow pleasantly in their souls, filling their lives with meaning and pleasant purpose far beyond other aspects of life.

SATAN'S WAR ON RESPONSIBLE FATHERHOOD

You have likely noticed an alarming decrease in emphasis on the importance of fathers in our society. Indeed, in a very real way, men are being relegated to a secondary role. They are often demeaned in the media and portrayed as clueless and inept. Or they are made to appear as exciting, womanizing heroes and role models, excelling in violence and sexual immorality. The days when men were cast in the role of righteous fathers and as a stable influence in the home in TV series and other media pretty much disappeared several decades ago.

Satan's way is that responsible fatherhood is a burden and limits freedom and options for immature self-indulgence and selfish satisfaction. Those who fall for the deceptions of the devil and his mortal subordinates regarding fatherhood set themselves up for ultimate lack of divine fulfillment and sell themselves short in eternal terms. And as far as mortal life is concerned, their conquests and self-indulgent activities ultimately flame out, leaving them lonely and in the cold ashes of misspent living.

THE LORD'S WAY

The Lord's way is that righteous fatherhood is, along with being a husband, the source of highest joy and satisfaction during mortality, as well as in eternity. We read in the Doctrine and Covenants that eternal parenthood is the essence of eternal godhood for worthy husbands and wives. Speaking of celestial marriage, the Lord said:

D&C 132:19–20

> 19 If a man marry a wife by my word, which is my law, and by the new and everlasting covenant, and it [temple marriage] is sealed unto them by the Holy Spirit of promise . . . [their marriage] shall be of full force when they are out of the world; and they shall pass . . . to their exaltation and glory in all things, as hath been sealed upon their heads, **which glory shall be a fulness and a continuation of the seeds forever and ever** [eternal parenthood].
>
> 20 **Then shall they be gods, because they have no end** [of posterity]. . . . Then shall they be gods, because they have all power, and the angels are subject unto them.

Thus, nothing could be a more worthy and desirable goal for men than being righteous fathers.

THE CLEAR INPUT OF MODERN "PROPHETS, SEERS, AND REVELATORS"

It is significant to note that the warnings and counsel given in the clearly prophetic proclamation on the family preceded by several years the now rapidly accelerating destruction of the family, with the accompanying de-emphasis on the role of fathers. That's what true prophets and seers do! They "see" ahead with inspired eyes and warn us in advance of dangers. Because of their prophetic foresight, we have a clear choice regarding fatherhood. We can choose the joy and satisfaction of righteous fatherhood or the sensual satisfaction and confused ups and downs of self-centered living, popularized by the media and being followed by multitudes in our culture and society. This tragic apostasy from righteous fatherhood, welcomed and promoted by many today, is doomed to ultimate failure. Whereas, those who patiently and continuously strive to learn and carry out the righteous role of fathers, according to God's plan, are destined by divine decree and the ever-present help of the Atonement to ultimately succeed.

HELPS FOR BEING RIGHTEOUS FATHERS

"The Family: A Proclamation to the World" provides goals toward which we can strive as husbands and fathers. It has specific guidance and terms that help sincere fathers succeed in their God-given role, including the following:

PRESIDE

The word *preside*, as used to describe one of the roles of fathers, must be handled very carefully. It must not be taken out of the context of the proclamation, which also includes the phrase "fathers and mothers are obligated to help one another as equal partners." How can one "preside" and still be "equal" with the other? The answer is simple. Husbands and wives are indeed equal partners in the Father's plan of happiness. In "presiding," the husband simply has the added responsibility to see that the mutual decisions of the "equal partnership" are carried out successfully. As an inherited gender trait, men tend to be more task-oriented, and it fits their competitive nature to ensure success in goals which are made by the partnership. An example may help.

In a ward organization, a bishop is called to preside. He participates in councils with other key leaders in the ward. Together, they set goals and make plans to achieve those goals so that all within the ward benefit from the Lord's plan of salvation. As the "presiding officer," the bishop has the responsibility to see that the plans of the councils are carried out. If he were to try to make all the plans and were to assume the role of "boss," riding roughshod over the desires and feelings of others, things would quickly fail and fall apart. Soon, it would be "Amen to the priesthood or the authority of that man" (D&C 121:37).

So also in the family unit. A father who is taking on the role of "boss" does not understand the word *preside*, nor does he understand the Lord's instructions to priesthood holders.

D&C 121:41–43

41 No power or influence can or ought to be maintained by virtue of the priesthood, only by **persuasion**, by **long-suffering**, by **gentleness** and **meekness**, and by **love unfeigned**;

42 By **kindness**, and **pure knowledge**, which shall greatly enlarge the soul **without hypocrisy**, and **without guile**—

43 **Reproving betimes with sharpness, when moved upon by the Holy Ghost; and then showing forth afterwards an increase of love** toward him whom thou hast reproved, lest he esteem thee to be his enemy.

And if he does not recognize the error of his ways and change, he soon becomes one who exercises the destructive power of "unrighteous dominion" (D&C 121:39.) "Preside" implies service. The Savior was the supreme example of one who presides. He served continuously. He gave His all for the blessing and comfort of others. Among other things, He washed the tired, dusty feet of weary apostles. He forgave and encouraged. He provided food and nourishment. Such is the model for the role of a righteous father and husband.

PROVIDER

A father's role as provider often requires that he make personal sacrifices in order to gain adequate education, training, and so forth, to provide a living for his family. Sometimes, a husband must choose to take or keep employment which does not provide as much money or personal satisfaction as he would like, yet does allow time for family. Such a choice can bring emotional security for his family and still provide a reliable income around which the family can carefully budget in order to meet basic needs and provide some extras. Some fathers keep "chasing rainbows" in a search for better or more interesting employment, to the extent that it becomes a way of life. They never settle down, thus leaving wife and children in a state of constant anxiousness about finances and security. Counseling together on this matter as husband and wife can be invaluable in helping the father fulfill his righteous role as described in the proclamation. Righteous fathers make tough decisions regarding time as well as money.

PROTECTOR

The role of "protector" can be viewed in many ways. Physical protection may not be as big an issue in developed nations as it was in times past. Providing adequate food, clothing, and housing is essential. Guarding and protecting the home and family from spiritual danger has become the real battlefront in most cases. Assuring that regular family prayer, scripture study, family home evening, and family councils are held, along with faithful church attendance, is a major part of a righteous father's role as a protector. In addition, fathers should be easy for wife and children to approach, whatever their needs might be. A father's laughter, smiles, and general pleasantness do much to provide a "protected" environment for his family.

IT TAKES TIME

It takes intentional setting aside of time for family to be a successful father. This is not always easy. For example, one of the busiest times in my career happened to be at the same time that our youngest was in Cub Scouts. As the time for the much anticipated Cub Scout rocket competition approached, it seemed that my work and Church responsibilities ratcheted up until my discretionary time was all but eliminated. Finally, the rocket contest was the coming Saturday morning, and I still hadn't found time to help Jared build his rocket. I was teaching institute of religion classes at the time and also supervising some special needs seminary programs. It was Thursday and, after teaching my classes at the institute, I was scheduled to meet at 4 p.m. with a special needs seminary principal to discuss plans for a new building. Just before my last afternoon Book of Mormon class, Jared called and asked if there was any possibility that we could work on the rocket kit when I got home from work. I told him what my schedule was, including some evening appointments at the stake offices, where I was serving as stake president, and assured him that we would get to it somehow. Dejectedly, he said, "OK, bye," and hung up.

Because of his phone call, I was almost late for class, so I hurried off to the classroom. Ironically, the lesson included discussing 3 Nephi 17:1–6, in which the Savior told the Nephite survivors of the destructions preceding His appearance to them that He must leave them and go to His Father as well as to the lost ten tribes. He assured them that He would be back to visit them again the next day. As He prepared to depart, the people yearned for Him to stay longer, verse 5, and, according to verse 6, He was filled with compassion for them and, consequently, altered His very busy schedule to respond to their needs and desires.

As I taught this segment in class, inviting student comments, I told them that my heart was deeply touched that one of the busiest people in the universe, who was, in fact, the Savior of "worlds without number" (Moses 1:33) and had so much to do, would drop what He was doing and tenderly spend more time ministering to these humble Nephites. As I said that, I was overwhelmed with guilt as I thought of my just-finished conversation with Jared. I felt like a hypocrite (which I was). I stumbled through the remaining minutes of class. As soon as I returned to my office, I called the special needs seminary principal and rescheduled that meeting. I then called my executive secretary and asked him to reschedule my evening appointments for a later date. Having done so, I called Jared and told him

I had rescheduled all my obligations for the evening and would be home in about a half hour to work with him on the rocket! He was thrilled, and so was I!

We worked together all evening. He carved the rocket's body from the balsa wood provided in the kit and painted it an ugly color (but it was his choice, and I complimented him on it). The kit contained a propeller, three thick rubber bands, and the necessary hooks for attaching the rubber bands to the propeller, as well as a bearing surface for the propeller against the front of the rocket body. According to the rules, it was optional to use all three rubber bands. I had purchased some extras for experimenting. We were told that the rules allowed soaking the rubber bands with glycerin to reduce friction when they were twisted together during winding up and unwinding.

At home, we experimented with how tightly we could wind the rubber bands before they broke. We bent a finishing nail into a hook shape so we could insert the pointed end into the chuck of a hand drill to make winding up the elastics easy. We found that we could wind them until they had three layers of "knots" before they broke. We were ready.

On the day of the contest, the Primary president and others were there to conduct the contest. Fishing line was strung between two hooks on opposite walls of a classroom. Each rocket came with two hooks, one in the front and one attached to the rear, on which it was to be suspended on the line, far enough below the line so that the propeller would not contact the fishing line as it slid along. As Jared's turn approached, he quietly said to me, "Dad, I've never won anything, and I know I won't win this, but thanks for helping me. It's been fun." My heart melted.

Several other cub scouts went first. Most of their rockets slid tentatively along the line. Some made it to the end at the opposite wall. A couple even picked up speed along the way. Then it was Jared's turn. With excitement, we carefully wound up the three attached rubber bands on his rocket clear to the max with our hand drill and hook. I warned him not to get a finger in the red plastic propeller because it was going to be very powerful. He grinned and said, "Yeah!"

He firmly gripped the propeller and the rocket, hooked it over the fishing line, and waited as the Primary president held her stopwatch in her hand and said, "Ready, set, go!" He let go and watched. The high torque of the triple-wound rubber bands spinning the propeller spun the whole rocket in a circle around the fishing line for a brief split second! We all held our breath. Then, in a blinding burst of tremendous propulsion, it rocketed across the room to win the competition in spectacular fashion, crashing into the wall and breaking into several pieces! He won!

It takes time to be a father. It takes intentionally setting aside both quality time and quantity time to be with family.

My own father was a busy man. Ours was a family of ten: Mom, Dad, and eight children. During our growing up years, he served twice as a bishop and several times on the high council. In addition to holding down a full-time job as an electrical engineer, he also did some consulting and other work on the side in order to provide for his family. Yet, he always had time for us kids. I well remember one of my sisters expressing gratitude for a father who took time to go on daddy-daughter dates with her, especially to daddy-daughter dances sponsored by our ward. She spoke of how wonderful it made her feel to be out on the dance floor, dancing with this tall, handsome man, her father, and how amazing it was to watch his large shoes as they moved so rhythmically around the dance floor, without stepping on her! The memory of dancing with her father still brings a thrill to her heart!

IT TAKES SENSITIVITY TO CHILDREN'S INDIVIDUAL NEEDS AND DESIRES

Fathers must intentionally be sensitive to the needs, individual personalities, wants, and desires of each of their children. Often this involves a wide range. One of my special memories is of Dad taking me with him to the company shop where employees were welcome to do after-hours work on their own projects. I was not yet in first grade and was always thrilled when he took me to the shop. He knew I was fascinated with machines and often let me accompany him, even though it slowed him down somewhat on his projects. I loved hearing other employees greet him and, even at my young age, recognized the genuine respect for him carried in their voices. One evening, I watched in fascination as he put some iron rod stock into a metal lathe and turned out a small, beautiful, shiny top for my little brother to use. He instilled a desire in me to learn how to do such things too.

I remember the time when I found an old, worn-out wheelbarrow tire that had been discarded in the town garbage dump. I was about five or six years old. It was a small community of perhaps two hundred people and was associated with a lead-zinc mine and mill in southeastern Nevada, essentially a company town. The dump was simply an area out away from town a bit, designated for garbage. We had hauled a load of junk and Dad shoveled it out of the trailer. While he did that, my older brother and I excitedly ran around looking for "treasures."

When I came upon the discarded wheelbarrow tire, my little boy's mind immediately thought, "Wow. My very own tire!" I picked it up, rolled it over to where Dad was, and excitedly said, "Dad! Look what I found! My very own tire!" Dad could very well have said, "David, for goodness' sake, put that down! Don't you see it is filthy? It is no good. That's why it is here!" But he didn't. He had already kindled in me a fascination with machinery and how things work. He had taught me about car tires and how they were inflated with air. He had let me try inflating a tire with a hand pump, but I was far too light to make it work. Then I watched as he did it and was very impressed. Instead of discouraging me, he looked at the tire with admiring eyes, smiled, and said, "Wow, that's quite a tire! Let me see you roll it." My child's heart swelled with pride that my dad liked my tire.

Children naturally seek approval from significant people in their lives, and a man who is aware of this and is willing to do whatever he can to be a good parent will be a far more effective righteous father. I of course didn't understand that my father was intentionally and by nature instilling in me an interest in mechanical things. Also, his confidence in me inspired self-confidence in myself. This is a vital trait of a good father. I took the tire home in the trailer and enjoyed it for a long time, rolling it around the yard, piling up dirt and making it climb up like I had seen Jeep tires climb up mountain roads during rides with Dad.

Once, I was chatting with our oldest son, Mike. He told me that he was harvesting a patch of potatoes in their large garden with his relatively small riding tractor. His young sons asked if they could drive it. He patiently, and with considerable pleasure as a father, taught each one how to work the controls and let them drive while sitting on his lap. Next time they visited our home, they excitedly told us that they had driven the tractor! He had created in them a "can do" attitude about themselves. In fact, he told us that they had assured him that now he wouldn't have to drive the tractor anymore because they could take over. He smiled at us and said, "They don't understand. That's not the point. I like to drive the tractor! It is not work!"

"LOVE THEIR MOTHER"

It seems that we have been hearing this wise counsel all our lives. It includes that we often express love to our wife, including in front of the children. I have heard it said to let your children "catch" you kissing in the kitchen! I like this counsel and strongly believe in it. Few behaviors on the part of fathers are more effective in creating a sense of security and belonging for children than observing and feeling the love their father has for their mother. This sense of well-being in their family is increased by many simple behaviors on the part of their father. For example, when they see their father bring flowers to their mother, when they see him holding their mother's hand, when they see him laughing and joking with her, and even flirting with her a bit—they can tell he loves their mother.

Dad created in me a strong desire to treat my wife with respect always. There was much pleasant exchange between Mom and Dad. He never raised his voice at her. He expressed his love for her often in front of us kids. I well remember one day when Mom, Dad, and I were driving from the family home in North Salt Lake, Utah, to downtown Salt Lake City. Our route included driving up Victory Road and then past the Capitol Building and down into the center of the city. We were all three occupying the front bench seat of the old Ford sedan we were driving. Just as we began the ascent up Victory Road, Dad reached over to Mom, took her hand in his, and addressed me, saying, "Dave, I just want you to know that your mother is everything I ever wanted in a wife. She is all my hopes and dreams in one." It was a simple gesture and statement, but it was indelibly impressed on my mind and remains clear and warm in my mind today. He created a powerful respect for womanhood and a strong desire in me to have such a marriage.

WHAT IF WE SUFFER SETBACKS AS FATHERS?

We know from the reality check of daily living that our best efforts at being good fathers do not always meet with success. Just ask Lehi. He and Sariah did their best to teach their children the ways of God and to provide a righteous home for their children. Sam, Nephi, Jacob, and Joseph (we don't have details about their daughters but know that they had some—see 2 Nephi 5:6) brought the joys and satisfactions of righteous fatherhood to Lehi. Laman and Lemuel brought sorrow and discouragement. Nevertheless, the Lord assured Lehi that he was saved (2 Nephi 1:15). And no doubt, Lehi felt a great deal of hope and comfort also as the spirit of prophecy came upon him and he blessed the posterity of Laman, Lemuel, and the sons of Ishmael that despite the waywardness of their parents, they would someday have the opportunity to partake of the blessings of the gospel (2 Nephi 4).

Furthermore, fathers in our day can take hope and comfort from the vision received by President Joseph F. Smith on October 3, 1918, with respect to children who rebel against the gospel lifestyle and do not repent during their lifetime. Speaking of the preaching of the gospel in the post-mortal spirit world, in the spirit prison portion of that realm, the vision teaches:

D&C 138:32

> 32 Thus was the gospel preached to those who had died in their sins, without a knowledge of the truth, or **in transgression, having rejected the prophets**.

Thus, it is clear from the scriptures that our Father in Heaven's plan of salvation includes a completely fair set of opportunities, under completely fair circumstances, for each individual, for all His children to understand and then accept or reject the gospel before final judgment.

Furthermore, President Wilford Woodruff, speaking of the temple work we do for our ancestors, taught: "There will be very few, if any, who will not accept the Gospel. . . . The fathers of this people will embrace the Gospel."[1]

This says a lot about the value of being taught the gospel under completely fair circumstances, such as in the post-mortal spirit world. And, if we correctly understand President Woodruff's quote above, it can no doubt apply likewise to wayward children who were excessively affected by peers, media, siblings, addictions, even unwise parenting, and so forth. The great comfort to parents is in knowing that such children will absolutely and ultimately get a fair chance to hear, understand, and accept or reject the gospel. After that, they will be able to exercise their agency fairly. Most will accept it and bring joy to their parents. Some will still reject it. But the burden will ultimately be lifted off the parents as their children's agency comes into full force.

IN SUMMARY

The wonder and beauty of the Father's plan includes making righteous fathers "co-creators" with Him in providing stable, righteous mortal homes for His spirit children. He has given fathers an endowment of father's intuition to nurture, protect, preside, and provide for their children. As we follow the abundant guidance of modern prophets, the scriptures, and the gift of the Holy Ghost, we can fully embrace the satisfaction and joy of righteous fatherhood.

NOTES

1. *Teachings of Presidents of the Church: Wilford Woodruff* (Church of Jesus Christ of Latter-day Saints, 2011), 191.

ABOUT THE AUTHOR

David J. Ridges taught for the Church Educational System for thirty-five years and taught for several years at BYU Campus Education Week. He taught adult religion classes and Know Your Religion classes for BYU Continuing Education for many years. He has also served as a curriculum writer for Sunday School, seminary, and institute of religion manuals.

He has served in many callings in the Church, including Gospel Doctrine teacher, bishop, stake president, and patriarch.

He and Sister Ridges have served two full-time CES missions together. They are the parents of six children and grandparents of twelve grandchildren so far. They make their home in Springville, Utah.